Business
Reimagined

Business
Reimagined

Why work isn't working
and what you can do about it

Dave Coplin

HARRIMAN HOUSE LTD

3A Penns Road
Petersfield
Hampshire
GU32 2EW
GREAT BRITAIN
Tel: +44 (0)1730 233870

Email: enquiries@harriman-house.com
Website: www.harriman-house.com

First published in Great Britain in 2013 by Harriman House.

ISBN: 9780857193315

British Library Cataloguing in Publication Data

A CIP catalogue record for this book can be obtained from the British Library.

Illustrations by DocktorBob

Set in Segoe and Dante MT

'As for the future, your task is not to foresee it, but to enable it.'

– ANTOINE DE SAINT-EXUPÉRY

For John, boldly go into your future
(and set your phaser to "stunning")

As a buyer of the printed book of *Business Reimagined*, you can download the full eBook free of charge. Simply point your smartphone or tablet camera at this QR code or go to:

ebooks.harriman-house.com/businessreimagined

Contents

About the Author

DAVE COPLIN is the Chief Envisioning Officer for Microsoft UK and an established thought leader in the UK. He has worked across a wide range of sectors and customers, providing strategic advice, leadership and guidance around the impact of technology on a modern society both at work and in play. Dave is passionate about turning the base metal of technology into valuable

Author photo © CTK Photobank/Rene Fluger

assets that affect the way that we live, learn, work and play and in so doing, move the focus from the technology itself to the actual outcome. Dave has contributed to a range of media articles, conferences and forums all relating to the goal of making technology less "visible" and more valuable in our daily lives.

www.theenvisioners.com | @dcoplin

Foreword
by Ben Hammersley

THE WORLD OF work is in a state of flux: there's an awful lot of uncertainty at the moment around how we should be working. If you believe the people that I write about and talk about and hang out with, the ones who claim to be making the future, the way we work and the places that we do it in are due an enormous amount of disruption.

Offices themselves, the architectural manifestation of work, are considered by many to be unnecessary; the view is that we have really cool cafés to work in instead. Offices have become a place of satire or even derision. Ricky Gervais only had to call his show *The Office* and we got the point without even seeing it.

Work and where we do it and how we do it really isn't cool any more, isn't worth talking about unless there are bean bags or table football tables. For many, paying attention to the way we work conjures up images of very dull men with clipboards and stopwatches. It's just not something that we want to do.

But I think we *should* be talking about work and the future because in fact it is incredibly useful, indeed it is necessary in this time of great change to look at these things; not in the "Hey everybody, let's live in Los Angeles and Skype in from the beach" way, but to examine the history of how we got here, the current trends and what is going to work in the future.

We need to examine the way that modern technologies have affected our lives and the way we work. We need to examine whether or not the way that we deal with those technologies, the way that we use them, the way that we buy them, the way that we handle them on a daily basis actually fits our expectations and needs.

In short we need to look at how we're being asked to work by the world at large and whether our existing systems might actually be preventing us from becoming more productive.

We have all heard the spiel, for example, about how having a completely open-plan office will foster huge amounts of collaboration or encourage huge amounts of knowledge-sharing; about how it will create a great deal of value for companies and for ourselves.

This isn't actually true.

So I think the time is right to reassess the way that we work against what it is we're actually trying to achieve. Collaboration is a very good thing and while collaboration tools, computers, the internet and social media are incredibly powerful and valuable, our work should be driven by achieving the best outcomes, not how best we can use the new cool tools.

Many of us – most of us – spend our lives in offices. We spend our lives doing knowledge work sat in front of a glowing rectangle. And too often, in my experience, we are obsessed in the modern workplace with simply getting on top of the problem. Instead we need to start getting to the bottom of it. Let's begin here.

Ben Hammersley
London, 2013

www.benhammersley.com | @benhammersley

Ben Hammersley is a technologist, writer and broadcaster. He is a contributing editor to the British edition of WIRED *magazine, the Prime Minister's Ambassador to TechCity, and Innovator in Residence at the Centre for Creative and Social Technologies at Goldsmiths, University of London. His latest book is* 64 Things You Need to Know Now For Then.

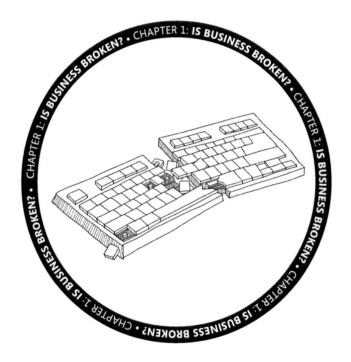

CHAPTER 1: **IS BUSINESS BROKEN?** • CHAPTER 1: **IS BUSINESS BROKEN?** • CHAPTER 1: **IS BUSINESS BROKEN?** • CHAPTER 1: **IS BUSINESS BROKEN?** • CHAPTER 1: **IS BUSINESS BROKEN?** •

SO LET'S GET this straight from the start: I meet all the stereotypes of someone who has dedicated his entire career to IT. I grew up on a healthy diet of *Star Trek* and comic books at the dawn of the personal computer revolution. I was taught (or wanted to believe) that technology could be a force for good in our society, that it would provide a set of tools which would enable us all to make the most of our potential.

And in many ways it seems that we are all living the dream. Our lives have been transformed by the advent of the internet and the web and the ever-faster evolution of connected devices and services. We have come an awfully long way in the last 40 years. In fact, we have come pretty far in the last four. And recent technological innovation, in particular, has tended to impact consumers more than businesses, turning our personal lives into rich technological experiences at almost every turn.

Whenever I am giving a speech as part of my job as a technologist, I ask people to raise their hand if the computer they have at home is better than the one in their office. Every single time, the majority of people have better technology at home. Normal people, not just geeks like me, have embraced technology in incredible ways. We are communicating with friends over Skype, we are playing games online, we are on Facebook, we are streaming movies and music and sharing photos. And we are doing all this increasingly on the move. It is worth pausing for a second to remember that only a decade ago the vast majority of people saw a computer as part of a place of work or study.

The technologists among us would say that the ever-accelerating trends of mobile, cloud, big data and social are transforming the IT landscape. Most of us would simply say that we live in a period where technology has become a normal, necessary part of our everyday lives.

But over the past few years a nagging sense of doubt has entered my mind about all this. I have begun to question the truth of the utopian vision of technology as the ultimate liberator. Like some people, I've been beginning to wonder whether the very thing that was supposed to set us free might not have instead ensnared us – without truly adding the value it promised.

Because there seems to be one area where technology fundamentally hasn't changed things. Work.

A recent study brought this into clear focus for me:

'Majority of American Workers Not Engaged in Their Jobs'

This was the headline that caught my eye. What sent me reeling was the detail. The study revealed that: '[s]eventy-one per cent of American workers are "not engaged" or are "actively disengaged" in their work, meaning they are emotionally disconnected from their workplaces and are less likely to be productive.'[1]

Seventy-one per cent? That means that less than a third of workers feel happy and productive in what they do, day in day out, 40 hours a week, 220 days a year.

Surely this cannot be true?

But I would guess that if you work as part of the knowledge economy inside any organisation, small or large, you will know for yourself that there is some foundation to this claim. It seems to be true of lots of companies in lots of countries; I did a bit of digging and found that these figures were replicated in the UK and many other developed nations.[2]

---

1 www.gallup.com/poll/150383/majority-american-workers-not-engaged-jobs.aspx

2 www.blessingwhite.com/content/reports/blessingwhite_2011_ee_report.pdf

Today we are living with the legacy of a couple of hundred or so years of office work. We have gone from working pretty much for ourselves (or the local lord) as farm workers and labourers, through the factories of the industrial revolution to working for big business with the rise of modern multinational corporations. And somewhere along the way, the way we work got stuck. We have found ourselves at the mercy of command-and-control hierarchies, butting up against principles that were designed for an analogue world and which have become more or less irrelevant in today's digital, connected world.

Everyone seems to agree that technology has changed everything. Then you look around at the world of work and realise that it really hasn't. There *are* superficial differences. Sometimes quite a lot of them. Yet, as we'll see, the underlying structure and principles of most people's working lives are the same as if the technological advances of the past quarter century had never taken place.

But is it technology that hasn't lived up to its promise or we who have failed to change to make the most of what's really on offer?

WORKING LIKE A VICTORIAN

We are living in a time of huge change but the way we work is still stuck in models first devised at the time of the industrial revolution. Let's take one aspect of work and follow it through by way of illustration.

Today we still reward work done in terms of time – hours worked. This owes itself to the industrial drive for business efficiency through standardisation: the production-line model of work where people perform a repetitive task or set of tasks contributing to an outcome or product, rather than creating an outcome or product themselves. This was the only way you could have scale. It was also the only way that you could make big, important things like steam trains or omnibuses.

This was a definite shift from the artisanal model of earlier times. What was being rewarded in this new way of work was not the outcome – an artefact sold at market – but hours spent on tasks. Workers received salaries for a working week based on clocking in and out. Companies focused on reducing the cost of labour and increasing the standardisation, all to improve the cost-efficiency and reliability of their manufacturing processes.

And so people became directly compensated for the *process* not the outcome of their work. This shift was very important. It didn't go away overnight. In fact, most of us are still living with it today.

As the industrial revolution came to an end and the knowledge revolution took hold – a development of the mid-20th century – the focus of most companies remained on driving business efficiency through standardisation.

The arena where this standardisation and efficiency took place became the office. It was the new place where workers swarmed around the provision of infrastructure.

In the industrial revolution, towns, cities and even countries prospered around the centralisation of infrastructure and resources, whether it was the dark satanic mills in Arkwright's Derbyshire or the mining towns of the valleys of South Wales.

This model carried on into the knowledge revolution because, in the pre-internet era of work, the only way to get the benefit of large-scale personal computing was in the office, where an IT department managed a network which all workers could utilise.

Offices became the very definition of productivity. But within all of this, the separation that had begun in the industrial revolution between employees and the outcome of their work was only widened.

For a while this disconnect was probably harmless enough. After all, products were being made, services were being offered, and many companies became wildly successful. But the levels of disengagement felt by the average knowledge worker today, and revealed in the studies earlier, should set alarm bells ringing.

Put simply: in a world where the reasons for swarming, standardisation and relentless focus on process are disappearing thanks to technology, continuing to organise our work around these principles is driving the majority of employees quietly mad.

THE ANTELOPE OF THE OPEN OFFICE

What we have lost in all of this is the fact that we are all, for the most part, professional, independent creative beings, employed by our firms to help them achieve great outcomes. Any process we are focusing on at a given time is just that: a process. If it is taken for the whole, the actual goal of our work – the ultimate outcome for our business – is lost. And that makes a business blind.

Things only get worse from there.

Employee discontent is not, of course, an entirely new problem. There have been efforts over the years to try and inject a sense of creativity into the office space, or to better enable collaborative work. Unfortunately, in the story of how the working world ended up such a disengaging mess, this is the bit where the good guys put together a brilliant scheme to save the day only to end up making things worse.

They came up with the open-plan office.

Unfortunately, open-plan offices just don't work very well. The theory is nice – remove physical barriers, make it easier to communicate – but the reality is awkward at best. Creative people forced into this type of work environment typically end up inventing new ways of creating barriers between themselves and their surrounding environment. Or they end up giving up on creativity.

Walk into any creative company – an advertising agency, say, or a publisher – and what you will see for the most part is row upon row of headphone-wearing creatives, all attempting to create a sense of personal space whilst remaining within the constraints of the business's idea of an environment that promotes creativity and collaboration.

For many creative industry employees and knowledge workers, headphones have become as essential a part of the corporate survival toolkit as cool laptop bags or hip personal phones.

Technology visionary Ben Hammersley describes this problem best when he refers to the 'hyper adrenalized' state of most open-plan workers. When placed in open-plan offices, argues

Hammersley, we become like antelope on the savannah, spending most of our time feeling vulnerable to the wide open nature of our habitat.

Everything we do is on display. It's hard for us to exert any kind of independent creative thought as we are simply part of a broader herd, surrounded by noise and chatter that only seeks to drive conformity not break it. Worse still, just like on the savannah, predators sit on the sidelines observing the herd, waiting for any individual to show signs of weakness. The antelope realise this and spend a vast portion of their time under significant stress from fear of attack.

Want to know where the power-brokers are on your floor? Look for the individuals who are placed around the edge looking in – facing the herd with their monitors shielded. I guarantee you, the people with this kind of geographic position in an office will be the power-brokers of your business.

Interestingly, the open-plan office again encourages a myopic focus on process over outcome. With everything they do in full view of everyone else, the employees in the middle of the office give up on creativity and settle for "productivity". While still valuable, this offers but a fraction of the full potential that they might actually bring to their employer.

Our centralised environments have effectively become cognitive wastelands, where flair and innovation are lost to the daily battle with outdated processes and forms of communication.

CAPTAIN KIRK'S INBOX

The modern day curse of email is a superb example of this insanity where productivity or process replaces creativity or work. It's also a great reminder of what happens when an outdated process (not email per se, but email for everything) is kept alive by successive waves of technology that enable its use to be both prolonged and perverted until the potential value it offers has been lost.

From all of the promises of the brighter technological future that *Star Trek* offered me as a kid, I never once recall Captain Kirk sitting on the Enterprise battling with his inbox. Or, for that matter, Captain Picard ignoring his bridge colleagues in favour of a sneaky peak at his communicator to see if that important message from the Romulans had come in.

So why, in the name of Spock, do so many of us now feel slaves to our email? We impulsively, constantly, fanatically check for messages when we should be cognitively elsewhere. We spend our lives on the merciless and never-ending quest for the nirvana of "inbox zero". Many of my friends (and yes, even myself) have, at some point, fallen victim to this way of thinking. We end up treating our mobile devices with disdain, blaming the fact we get email rather than blaming ourselves for checking for messages every five minutes.

It's a classic example of where technology becomes the prison rather than the release.

I'm not calling for the death of email. It remains one of the core foundations of our digital communication toolbox. But we have allowed it – like so many other tools before – to become the *only* solution when so many other, better choices exist.

After all, when you think about it, email exists for three important reasons:

1. It is precise in its targeting – it is sent to only those recipients we choose.

2. It is primarily asynchronous in operation, i.e. it is not (and was never) designed to be a real-time form of communication.

3. For some bizarre reason, it remains the only communication tool that is consistently cached by devices – i.e. you can access your inbox and send messages even if (God forbid) you are without a network connection. This alone makes it the lowest common denominator of the digital communication world.

Today, every single member of our digital society has an email address. They *may* be contactable by other channels, but if I want to be sure I can reach them, and if the communication is not time-critical, email is the perfect medium.

The problem is, though, that most of the emails we receive don't fulfil those criteria. Our inboxes are full of communications that should have been sent through more appropriate means or should never have been sent at all. Email is not really designed for organisation-wide messages, or for messages requiring immediate attention; nor is its "reply all" button actually meant to be used to supply everyone with an endless stream of jokes, organisational showmanship and pointless grandstanding.

All of the above may have been fine when all we had for communicating digitally was email, but that's just no longer the case. There are dozens of different tools out there, each suited to a different kind of need.

So why if we have all this choice do we find it so hard to change?

EXPERIENCE VS. INNOVATION

As humans we are pretty much defined by our past experiences. This is as true for us as a society as it is for us as individuals. When confronted with new technology, offering new experiences, we typically end up using it much the same way as the old technology it has replaced.

One of the best examples of just how hard it is for humans to adapt to the opportunities afforded by new technology sits unassumingly below our fingertips every single day. The QWERTY keyboard layout is one of the classic designs of our time, and yet its main reason for existing has long since passed.

The QWERTY keyboard layout was invented in 1867 and, although the exact reasons for its creation are somewhat contested, both sides of the argument concede it was a solution to a problem we simply no longer have. Depending on who you believe, Morse code telegraph engineers needed to minimise mistakes, or office typists needed to stop the mechanical heads on their typewriters from jamming when they typed too quickly. QWERTY proved perfect and caught on. And we have been stuck with it ever since, even though it has been proven to be slower, clumsier and less intuitive than any number of alternatives invented since then.

We are surrounded by incredible advances in personal computer technology. Most of us walk around with more computing power in our pockets than was on our desks a few short years ago. We live in a world of touchscreens, voice and gesture interfaces … and we still type like we're in the 1880s.

As I said, it is not as if the QWERTY keyboard layout has not been improved on many times since its inception. Perhaps the most famous alternative is the DVORAK keyboard, designed just 80 years ago, when mechanical typewriter engineering had progressed somewhat.

Unlike its predecessor, the DVORAK layout was primarily built for speed. Its middle row of letters – the home row – uses all five vowels and the five most common consonants: AOEUIDHTNS. With this layout, the home row letters perform around 70% of all the work, making it possible to type 400 of the English language's most common words without leaving the row where your fingers naturally rest.

With the QWERTY layout, the home row provides just 32% and 100 of the most common words.

All these advantages, and yet the DVORAK never caught on. There are several reasons why QWERTY still rules supreme – standardisation being one of the most powerful – but the basic underlying cause is simply human inertia. In other words, we like what we know and we know what we like.

The subtext to this is incredibly important, especially for those of us in the technology industry. It means that in all the challenges facing an unreformed and unproductive working world, technology itself is in many respects the *least* of those challenges.

If you cannot help people to change, technology changing all around them won't make the slightest difference.

THE PROBLEM OF PRODUCTIVITY

Our definition of productivity – office-bound, process-focused, unimaginative – lies at the very heart of our problems here. We've applied technology to solve the problem of productivity, we've created processes to solve the problem of productivity and we're even using offices to solve the problem of productivity.

Productivity is in danger of becoming the curse of the modern day workplace. We have become transfixed by improving productivity to such an extent that we are starting to forget the other attributes that most people bring to their organisations every single day. We spend our working days locked to a single period of time and a single physical location, batting communications back and forward in a sort of nightmarish game of digital ping-pong. Success is defined by the number of individual processes we complete not the outcomes of the organisation.

The massive risk here is that in a world defined by its processes and not its outcomes, working *smarter* is not an option and the only feasible alternative is simply to work *harder*. This, in a nutshell, is the core of why I think work isn't working.

CREATIVE BUSINESSES ARE THE FUTURE

Chasing the dragon of productivity undermines our potential contribution as employees and robs organisations of the potential for innovation. Chaining ourselves to processes and the open-plan, bums-on-seats style of collaboration makes it much harder for us to tap into the incredible potential of people. But why is this important for organisations – and why now?

It's important because the industrialised world is reaching a point of parity, where improving the quality or quantity of products and services is less and less able to provide organisations with the competitive advantage they need to be successful (or even survive). In this "post-informational" world, as it's been called, our attention must now turn to creativity.

What is most important now is the ability of organisations to think differently about what they do. What counts is how they adapt to new opportunities and innovations.

The problem is, of course, that this is a world that our past experiences have not prepared us for. Our office spaces are neither conducive nor relevant to it. Our process-driven work culture is too rigid and narrow for it. And employees are simply not equipped with either the latitude or the cultural ability to adapt to it.

HOW CREATIVITY WORKS

Psychology helps us understand what we need to do to promote this new level of creative connectivity. As business psychologist Tony Crabbe points out, creativity tends to divide into three general categories of activity:

1. intellectual ambling

2. connecting brains

3. deep thinking.

Intellectual ambling is a solitary activity where the brain is allowed to wander, ruminate and explore. Fundamentally, the brain is a connection-making machine. Any new learning or creative insight occurs when a new pattern of connections is made. However, it is easy to stop these connections from happening. Think of a time when you were trying to solve a really difficult problem, or come up with a great idea. Often we get the feeling we are not far from our solution. What's happening at that point is the brain is grasping, straining to hear the weak signals from distant synapses. In fact, vision is such a dominant sense, when we are close to an insight, the brain floods the visual cortex with alpha waves to shut it up so it can focus on making the connection. This means that, for about 0.3 of a second before we have an insight, we tend to go blind!

Our current workplaces, which prioritise activity over thought, reaction over reflection make intellectual ambling counter-cultural. Even more significantly, the noise and distractions make listening for insights extremely difficult: either from the chaos of meeting after meeting, or the incessant flow of email after email, or the office chatter going on around us. We have effectively created insight-preventing workspaces.

Connecting brains. Creativity happens when new connections between ideas are made. Why do those ideas need to be in a single head? Connecting brains is a social activity that involves discussing, sharing and brainstorming with others. The notion that we will increase creativity if we allow people to work with others, to share thinking and perspectives is not new. In fact, you could argue, the primary objective of the open-plan office is to facilitate serendipitous encounters between people and ideas. The more diverse the connections, the greater the propensity to make new connections, and therefore the more likely it will be that innovations will follow.

But again, the current workplace runs counter to this, and not simply in the antelope-effect of open-plan offices that we discussed earlier. The problem is we surround ourselves by like-minded people working on similar problems. Where possible, we need to broaden and extend the cognitive gene pool of our organisations. We are less likely to make new discoveries or to discover truly disruptive innovation when we are stuck in open-plan teams or organisational pods of people who are more or less doing exactly the same kind of work as us and see the world in exactly the same way. "Group think" is a classic symptom of our problem. If the intent is to generate some genuinely new thinking, it is going to happen much less often with people who see the world the same way as you.

Deep thinking might not sound the most "creative" type of approach; it is more grunt than flair, where solutions are ground out through concerted intellectual effort. Deep thinking needs time and focus. The problem here is establishing both the time and the environment that even allows *deep thinking* to take place. According to experts, it takes the average human around 15 minutes to achieve "flow state" thinking, the place where our cognitive powers are at their most powerful. Yet the chances of finding 15 contiguous minutes in our current working environments without interruption from meetings, emails or other distractions are so rare that we are unlikely to ever harness this incredible power. Multi-tasking has become the order of the day for all employees, and yet studies have increasingly proved that focusing on multiple tasks simultaneously makes us 30% less effective than if we focus on each one in turn.

So the proposition of this book is that the workplace is no longer fit for purpose. In a world that requires greater creativity we need to take a more flexible approach to both the workplace and the work we do. Successful businesses will be those that can provide the physical *and* cognitive space needed for their employees to flourish, with employees becoming creative individuals committed not to aimless productivity or repetitive processes but on helping their organisations achieve their aims.

How will we get there? We're going to have to start reimagining business.

CHAPTER 2: **GETTING FLEXIBLE** • CHAPTER 2: **GETTING FLEXIBLE** • CHAPTER 2: **GETTING FLEXIBLE** • CHAPTER 2: **GETTING FLEXIBLE** • CHAPTER 2: **GETTING FLEXIBLE** • CHAPTER 2: **GETTING FLEXIBLE** •

THE MAN WITH NO OFFICE

MIKE DEAN IS a relatively rare example of a truly flexible worker. He works for high-powered consulting firm Accenture as head of its business process outsourcing unit for the UK, Ireland and the Nordics. He is responsible for 900 staff and business worth hundreds of millions of pounds.

But he does not have an office.

Instead he divides his time between client visits and working from home. What's more, he only works three days a week. The rest of the time he helps to run youth groups and enterprise projects in schools.

Accenture's leadership recognised a few years ago that the culture of long hours in the office and presentee-ism was not going to attract and retain the sort of talented individuals required in today's marketplace.

'Luckily a few of us who felt very strongly about this managed to get our voices heard and explain that a) the old way of working wasn't a sustainable model and b) it certainly wasn't a model that was attractive to the next generation of the people we wanted to get on board. And Accenture at the senior leadership level absolutely got this,' Mike says.

He calls it 'working smarter' and on a personal level he says he has to be ultra-organised to maintain this level of flexible working. He spends a couple of hours on a Monday planning the week in detail, only heading into head office in London perhaps once a month. When there, it is rare for him to have meetings. Instead he spends those moments catching up with colleagues. 'You end up spending the whole day with conversations that usually start with "Oh Mike, I haven't seen you for a while. How are you doing?" and that's great.'

Technology has enabled this way of working. 'I don't have any papers anymore. I have no filing cabinet because it's not necessary. I carry everything in a little rucksack: I've got a PC, I've got a smartphone and I've got a time manager where I keep my list of things that I need to do, and a day book. And that's it. I can go anywhere, be anywhere – it is very much a mobile lifestyle.'

But there are cultural hurdles to be overcome both at Accenture and in the wider business community, Mike says.

'There are people who feel that if you work from home or work flexibly, you will be marked down as less committed, second class, not prepared to put the work in, a bit of a shirker. It's that that we've got to overcome. I think we're making huge strides and I think in another five or six years we will wonder what the fuss was ever about.'

Mike Dean is but one of a small but growing number of workers who have discovered the transformational advantages of stepping out of the structure of traditional office work – advantages which accrue both to the employee and their employer. His experiences help to highlight not just the benefits flexible working can bring but the significant obstacles that have to be overcome in order to fully realise it.

Indeed, there is still a lot of confusion among businesses and workers as to what really flexible working actually is.

TRUE FLEXIBLE WORKING

I know companies who have been talking about the potential for flexible working for years. The real challenge in this conversation is not so much whether a firm is for it or against it, but in extending the horizons of what they think might be possible. All people hear is "working from home". While this is obviously a key component of what flexible working offers, this simplistic understanding actually misses the point and belittles the true potential of an authentically flexible approach.

At its core, genuine flexible working is pretty simple. It just means being thoughtful about the tasks you have to achieve each day and choosing the most appropriate location from which to accomplish them. This is where the transformation happens, where work no longer is defined by a specific location, but instead is simply an activity, something you do.

Flexible working is about being able to be effective regardless of your location; whether that's at home, in the airport, on the train, in a café, or at a specially designed drop-in office. It's also about being effective *because* of your location. You might need to be closer to customers; or you might need space for deep thinking. Flexible working lets you accomplish either with minimal fuss. It is most definitely *not* an employee perk or HR arrangement made for individuals based on their personal preferences or situation.

To realise the full potential that flexible working can bring, industry and government need to invest in creating "third spaces" that allow people to meet and be productive without crowding onto train platforms at half past seven in the morning. There is a huge opportunity to make better use of our high streets, empty shops, moribund pubs, libraries and other community sites, reinventing them as places that let workers plug in, connect and collaborate.

Why do so many of us endure the humiliation of commuting, spending huge amounts of time and money in order to be in the same place, with the same people, at the same time, every working day? We no longer need to congregate around central organisational hubs to work. The infrastructure that used to be solely available there is now dispersed and for the most part can be found in our pockets, laptop bags, coffee shops and local libraries.

Moving people around en masse every single working day feels like an outdated 20th century approach to a task that could be easily bettered by 21st century thinking. Notwithstanding the huge environmental benefits, flexible working should also mean that we spend more time (and money) in our local communities, thereby shifting resources back towards smaller cities, towns and villages.

Of course, we will still need to travel. We will still visit the central hubs of business and commerce in our regions. But the point is we should visit them less. We should have a choice. We should reap the rewards when we use them, rather than using them by default.

Under this new definition, flexible working represents a way of working that goes far beyond traditional remote-working and embraces new work styles. It is designed to encourage organisations to free their people to work in the ways which allow them to be most productive. It is part of the much-needed shift towards measuring employees by outputs not inputs.

SMARTER, BETTER COLLABORATION

Of course, in exploring the potential that technology affords it's incredibly easy (and dangerous) to jump to extremes. Flexible working does not mean that it's fine for people to work permanently in isolation. After all, the best ideas are often a cumulative effort, spawned by shared thoughts and multiple opinions.

So it is crucial that employees are able to match tasks to environments and environments to people. Sometimes it helps to have someone who understands the context of your challenge to act as a sounding board. Sometimes the only way to break through barriers to reach true innovation is to bump up against people who *don't* understand the context. Even in our hyper-connected society, it is difficult to replicate the level of connection made when speaking to someone face to face. On the other hand, there are some jobs that require focus and are best tackled away from the chaotic hubbub of the office. The point is that different people find inspiration in different places and they should be empowered to choose to work from wherever they are most productive, rather than simply choosing between the office and home.

According to a new study on flexible working commissioned by Microsoft, a massive 70% of office workers say they can get 'more done' working away from the office. Critically, over one third (38%) say they can be more creative when they are able to work flexibly. The head of the Law Society in the UK called on firms to expand flexible job arrangements to help more women reach the top. Lucy Scott-Moncrieff said forcing staff to work conventional hours of nine to five damaged creativity and innovation and made it harder to attract and retain talented working mothers and others.

So why, in the face of all of this, is it so hard for individuals and organisations to embrace flexible working?

INFLEXIBLE ABOUT FLEXIBILITY

Research commissioned by the Anywhere Working Consortium suggests that flexible working is being held back by trust – or rather, a lack of it. But it's not what you might expect.

It isn't that bosses fear their staff are putting their feet up at home. It's that employees are terrified that their bosses or fellow workers will think they are. Why? Because that's what they think of others.

According to the study's findings, nearly three quarters (73%) of the British workforce believes that remote workers will not work as hard as office-based staff. This was identified as the biggest barrier to working anywhere. Not having access to the right technology – the classic reason for offices, don't forget – was cited by just 24% as an issue.

This is pretty incredible. Firstly, it shows once again that technology is not the barrier any more. Secondly, it also shows that the biggest issue we face in making business more effective and engaging for the information age is the *human* element.

An Ipsos MORI study on flexible working highlights some of the other eminently human anxieties getting in the way.

They found that individuals working away from the office feel under pressure to overcompensate for their absence. In order to quash colleagues' negative perceptions, nearly half (47%) make a conscious attempt to be extra visible by sending more emails and making more phone calls. Almost one in three (30%) feel guilty about not being in the office, with over a third (39%) working longer hours to prove they are not "shirking from home".

So even when flexible working is in place, it can be quite as destructive as the most regimented, process-driven, anxiety-filled open-plan office. Without a deeper cultural change, in fact, it's useless.

Philip Ross, CEO of workplace consultancy Unwork, brings this startling reality into perspective. Even when not present in an office, he notes, 'there is a risk that workers will prioritise presentee-ism over effectiveness'.

BUMS ON SEATS

So flexible working is great, but the people first in line to benefit from it – employees – mistrust it. And even those who go ahead and embrace it are often so paranoid about others' mistrust that they aren't doing it properly.

But employers haven't helped either. There's more than enough misunderstanding to go around. This was brought into sharp relief by Marissa Mayer's decision to call an end to Yahoo!'s working-from-home policy.

When the memo sent by Yahoo!'s head of HR dropped into the inboxes of staff, there was uproar both inside and outside the organisation. The memo stated:

> 'Some of the best decisions and insights come from hallway and cafeteria discussions, meeting new people, and impromptu team meetings. Speed and quality are often sacrificed when we work from home.'

It is speculated that the move to get staff back into the office from June 2013 was driven by Mayer, who herself returned to work weeks after giving birth. But whatever the business motives behind the move, many reacted strongly. Even Virgin entrepreneur Richard Branson had something to say on the matter, calling it a 'backwards step in an age when remote working is easier and more effective than ever'.

This kind of "bums on seats" memo is often sent out by organisations when they feel their flexible working policy is being abused by employees. And it's a classic indicator that true flexible working was never really being considered, let alone practised.

Too often, flexible working is brought in on an individual basis. It's an ad-hoc measure. Sure, the organisation may have some blanket policy that makes it acceptable; but mostly it is down to individual negotiation, typically with the HR department. Again, this misses the potential of flexible working by more than a country mile. Why? Because it ensures that the rest of the organisational changes that are required to make flexible working successful are never implemented.

Domestic arrangements are perceived to be the driving force behind establishing flexible working. But did you know that only 22% of people surveyed (Ipsos MORI) cited childcare as the main reason for working away from the office? Even pro-flexibility employers are getting it wrong in all sorts of ways. Many flexible working policies exist merely as a means of accommodating parents' responsibilities. Laudable, of course. But something that at no point considers the *potential* of the policy – or even thinks of it as anything other than a necessary evil.

BEING STRATEGIC

Flexible working should be seen by organisations as a *strategic operational objective*. It is not so much about accommodating employees (though that's great). It's actually about unlocking their full potential. And it's one of the most significant things any business can do to improve its long-term success.

Sure, if companies do it and do it well, they will have happier employees who achieve more and have better work-life balance – but that will simply be a by-product, a side effect, not the actual objective.

The reason authentic flexible working is so transformative is that companies which take a comprehensive approach to flexible working have to re-orient their entire way of working around this new model. This means doing away with the days of productivity standardisation and a relentless focus on the component processes that go into making products and services. Taking their place is an outcome-focused approach that ensures that every single employee is empowered to be responsible for their part in the success of their organisation.

Organisations that adopt this strategic approach to flexible working will stand a greater chance of success not just because they have changed their culture and objectives to ones that unlock and reward the natural entrepreneurialism of their employees. They will also have addressed the key issue of trust. By focusing on the outcome for the organisation rather than the individual the *entire* trust dynamic changes.

If flexible working is adopted on an individual-by-individual basis then the disparity between employees that will inevitably come into being will lead to trust issues. Not so much between employee and employer (though it happens), but worse: between employees. If employees are instead empowered to work flexibly in order to contribute to the overall success of the organisation, they assume far greater responsibility in their role (and the roles of their co-workers) and the issue of trust all but disappears.

Meanwhile, performance goes through the roof. Particularly when it's helped by advances like those we'll see in the next chapter.

CHAPTER 3: **BEING SOCIAL** • CHAPTER 3: **BEING SOCIAL** • CHAPTER 3: **BEING SOCIAL** • CHAPTER 3: **BEING SOCIAL** • CHAPTER 3: **BEING SOCIAL** • CHAPTER 3: **BEING SOCIAL** •

SOCIAL WIZARDRY

RICHARD PATTERSON'S BUSINESS is built on understanding what his customers are saying and what his customers' customers are saying. A few years ago he realised that they were increasingly using social networks, blogs and forums to make themselves heard. It turned his business on its head.

Richard is the CEO of Merlin, an IT and consumer services company based in Buckingham. He founded the company with his partners in 1991 and has grown it into a global business with 400 employees and operations in the Far East, Europe and the US.

The company's clients include blue-chip financial and healthcare firms – companies including General Electric, DHL and Emerson.

Merlin's DNA is built on great customer service and IT support. In about 2007, early on in the growth of social networks, Richard and his colleagues began to realise that customers were deserting traditional forms of communication. They were switching to social media to talk about customer issues.

So it was a business imperative for Merlin to understand social networks and to develop business tools based around their principles for clients.

'Ultimately,' says Richard, 'if you're going to deliver a professional customer support service, you need to allow the consumer to communicate with you in the way they want to communicate. If not, you're going to miss your whole customer base.'

So back in 2007, Merlin started incorporating social elements into its own business. By 2009 this had led to the company implementing the private social network technology of Yammer, then a standalone product (since acquired by Microsoft) throughout the business.

Internally, becoming a business with built-in elements of social networking had one immediate effect – the disbanding of

Merlin's internal IT support desk, replaced by the company's socially-enabled "big brain".

'We believe that the help desk is on a limited life,' says Richard. 'What you need is somebody with a big brain, somebody who knows everything about everything. The reality is those people don't exist. But through things like social networking, you can create a virtual big brain. In other words, out there in the organisation there is probably somebody that knows about the problem you have. All you've got to do is find a way of connecting the person who has the problem with the person who knows the answer. Social networking is exactly that platform.'

The company's "Ask Me" group means that 'wherever I am in the world, if I have a question, I can be pretty certain that somebody will answer it for me within a couple of hours,' says Richard. 'It may be support within the company, or it may be somebody else who's experienced exactly the same thing. This is collaboration in practice, and it's working for real within our business.'

Social is also helping Merlin reimagine its services and how its business will develop in the future. 'Probably 50% of our business is based around being an IT help desk and if I've just proven that I can do away with the help desk for my company, then I need to be able to understand what's going to happen to my business over the coming years,' Richard says.

So social is powerful stuff – and it's going to be doing a lot of reshaping of the world of work as we know it. Or, of course, a lot of businesses are going to end up left behind …

WHAT IS A SOCIAL ENTERPRISE?

The terms "social enterprise" and "social business" are pretty hotly contested these days. That's made them both a little tainted and confused. The truth is, like all of these things, they mean different things to different people.

And that's mostly fine. Just as there is no single right way for organisations, brands or individuals to do social media, so there is no single right way to be a social business. However, there are some key principles that set apart those that understand it more than others. And these can definitely determine a firm's success.

The first thing to understand is that being a social business is *not* about how well you "do" social to bridge the relationship between your organisation and your customers. In other words, it's not about how helpful your tweets are (though naturally I hope they are helpful). That should be to your business as breathing is to a human being. It's just a basic function you need to perform to survive – and thankfully one that has been written about at length in many other places.

The proper definition of social business is much, much more. It is, like Richard and Merlin have found, a way of going beyond how your firm currently works. It's a way of fundamentally changing the way you do business. It's got nothing to do with incremental advances – "doing the same stuff a bit better". Instead it's all about the scary, white-knuckle, leap-of-faith sort of transformation that generates true change and new opportunities.

Switching off your help desk takes a lot of confidence. You can't do it in isolation, on the whim of a few leaders or with a handful of "social activists" inside your organisation. The same is true of any other business going social. The technological change has to be matched with a cultural one.

A social business is one that recognises that its greatest value is how its people are connected to each other and how in turn they are connected to the people they serve inside and outside the business. It's one that truly recognises the value of simply bringing people together and giving them an outcome you want them to achieve.

AN ALMOST ELEMENTAL FORCE

Over the past ten years, social networks have been slowly democratising the way our society communicates. Often quite radically, they've enabled citizens to engage with communities at local, national and global levels to affect real change in how they are governed. And of course, more simply, they've enabled friends, family and fans to stay connected and engaged. Social has proved itself to be a powerful, almost elemental, force.

By its nature, social flattens the old communication hierarchies. It offers the sort of scale, breadth and velocity that simply cannot be matched by any other means. And this is key to its power in all sorts of ways. The opportunity for disruption (both positive and negative) is as great for businesses as it is for governments and individuals. Social powered the Arab Spring. It engages citizens and governments. It has created (and in some extreme cases, destroyed) businesses and individuals.

Most importantly, for this chapter's focus, it means that every single employee and every single customer has both a voice and a direct line with those who can affect real change in a business's services or products.

Social is democratic. And it's thoroughly human. It provides a rich, warm, human signal in a world filled with the cold, dark, binary logic of corporate processes and computer algorithms. Twenty years ago, if you wanted to engage with a business as a consumer, it would take a formally worded letter. Ten years ago that same letter would have been sent via email. Today, you deliver the same message to businesses on first-name terms and usually in fewer than 140 characters.

This new way of communicating has brought new expectations about how individuals and organisations communicate with each other. It has spawned a whole new branch of etiquette. At this point we would do well to remember that this sort of change is in fact nothing new in itself; we had the same debates as a society when emails started to take over from printed letters (and for that matter, when printed letters took over from handwritten letters). What is new, though, is the tone of "personality" that is expected within social communication.

Until now, if you wanted to interact with a business you would have to work your way through the customer services department, or the hierarchy of the part of the business you were dealing with. Today, you can get directly to the individual responsible for what you are interested in. You can likely also get a sense of the human behind the role. All of this helps to speed things up and focus communication. Equally, it exposes the inefficiencies of the old formality. Mercifully the ancient, sclerotic days of *Dear Sir/Madam* and *To whom it may concern* are almost behind us.

FLATTENED AND FRICTIONLESS

Another knock-on effect of this way of communicating is that it completely flattens the informational and organisational hierarchies that exist both within and outside an organisation. Although ultimately it is about reducing the friction in communicating between people, this also offers significant additional benefits.

For example, in email, addressing and permissions are the same thing. If I want you to be able to see it, I have to send it to you. In social, they're different things. I can send something to you but enable another group of people to see it.

Huge benefits come from subtle capabilities like this. Ultimately it means that all of the information that used to be locked up in siloed communications can be opened up to people that may need that information, whether they need it when the message is first conveyed or at *any point in the future*.

And with social tools it is easier to organise quickly. You can find the people you need, get them into a group, accomplish something and then move on. Meanwhile you have left a trail of what was accomplished so that, as people come and go, they can use that information – and perhaps further interaction – to affect real change of their own.

There is one last important benefit of social's democratisation of the workplace. This is what some have called giving a voice to the voiceless in business.

Although many of the examples so far have been focused around the knowledge workers inside an organisation, it would be a mistake to think that all of the benefits (and challenges) I've described are only applicable to them. Naturally knowledge workers are the easiest to connect up in a network. But in reality, knowledge workers are a minority in many businesses.

In retail, for example, there's a movement right now among really large companies to give a voice to non-knowledge workers. Almost everyone has a smartphone now – a computer in their pocket – and that means everyone can be connected at work. So everyone can have a voice that can affect their company's operations in a way that simply was not possible until now. That ability to empower your workforce and tap into the hidden potential of employees in every part of the enterprise is truly exciting.

A hamburger chain in the US recently introduced social sharing within the company, empowering local store managers to create and share ideas on how to get customers to spend more at the bar to reverse flagging profits. Soon stores began to put experiments into place. Turnover noticeably improved. Even better, the stores that experimented also reported lower staff turnover. You ask your employees to help you solve a problem, you get them aligned – and it turns out they're a lot more effective and engaged.

WHAT SOCIAL MEANS FOR YOUR BUSINESS

If you boil it all down, social networks are just communication tools. But they are brilliantly subtle, powerful, fully featured tools. They offer a way of wiring your people together better than they ever have been.

Using them – and the principles they embody – will necessarily make you move faster. It will allow you to be more agile. And it will allow people to be more engaged in what they're doing.

So the social business is just about adding another communication tool?

Well, not quite. That's a hugely powerful part of it. But just like flexible working, merely making it available is not enough.

We have to remember the human element and the importance of culture.

A social business is about more than just communication tools. If it is anything, it is an embodiment of a philosophy. It is a new, more active, democratic kind of business from top to bottom.

Adding another communication channel does not itself make your business more effective. You could put a second telephone on your desk but it wouldn't make you any more effective.

If your organisation never uses a telephone, even putting a single telephone on your desk won't help you. In fact, it might drag you down. You could end up adapting your working day to being chained to your desk waiting for it to ring – or fending off cold-callers.

What makes you more effective as an organisation isn't new tools (powerful and great as they are). It's changing so that everyone uses the tools. With a social business that means helping people understand the value of drawing on the network rather than just the people that they know. It is the single most effective technical solution of directly connecting everyone inside and outside of your organisation.

Here's a great example of it. Research and development is a key area where social collaboration is having huge impact. In industries like pharmaceuticals the product lines are so large in terms of revenue that all you have to do is move the needle by tiny amounts and you've made a very significant impact on the bottom line.

Filtering new ideas in these businesses is critical, so if you introduce something that allows collaboration and openness between disparate parts of the research teams, it can quickly pay off.

I have been told about one thread on a defence contractor's network that went along these lines: 'Hey, we're about to do some research into this topic.' And the first response was, 'Hey, we're six months done researching into that topic. Here's our findings so far. Maybe we can work together.' And then somebody replied and said, 'We did this research two years ago. Here's the findings. Can we just stop doing it now?'

A QUICKER WAY OF MOVING

'The business case for social is agility, pure and simple.'

– MIKE GRAFHAM, YAMMER

Agility is the ability to respond to stuff changing. For most businesses, if a change takes place (internally or externally), they tend to get together a group of people to try and get on top of it and come up with a decent response.

This is, of course, a really slow way of doing things.

Firstly you have to understand that something has changed. That's not always quick or easy. Secondly you need to get a group of people together that understand the change. Again, easier said than done. Then they need to be able to understand (and agree) what the business has to do in order to either take advantage of the change or avoid the thing that's about to hit them.

Then, at long last, you align your business to make its response.

A social business changes that. Having a very well networked organisation allows you to identify and react to changes better because the first person to observe it now has a mechanism for immediately getting it under as many people's noses as is relevant. They have a reliable mechanism for bringing it to the attention of people who actually care about it.

You then also have a better mechanism for getting the word out to others when you need to shape and finally implement your response.

In a sense, social is about broadening the cognitive gene pool of your organisation, harnessing the wisdom of the crowd.

It's not just more effective communication – it changes the information-sharing dynamics inside a business by ensuring that information can flow as fast and free as the ideas.

SOCIAL STUMBLES

But if the benefits of being social are becoming well-known, why are so many businesses struggling to implement it?

The road to the social business is littered with the failures of past corporate projects and initiatives, all undoubtedly well-intentioned but mostly doomed to failure. Gartner research found that 'although social technologies are employed by 70% of organisations, most social collaboration initiatives fail because they follow a worst-practice approach of "provide and pray", leading to a 10% success rate.'[3]

While this is a shocking statistic, it says more about the challenge of the kind of human change required than the problems associated with the technology.

Social business initiatives usually fail for a few simple reasons:

1. **Social collaboration is disruptive by its very nature.** It tramples over organisational boundaries, corporate status and the sort of stale business etiquette that has been around for decades. It cannot be adopted in isolation – it represents, and therefore requires, a significant cultural change, not just in individuals but across the entirety of an organisation. Just like the problem of flexible working being thought about in the context of specific individuals rather than

---

3 **www.gartner.com/newsroom/id/2402115**

for the benefit of an entire business, many social business projects are adopted only within teams or departments, leaving the rest of the organisation untouched. Even when implemented company-wide, social is often implemented in isolation, or alongside other existing processes. As a result the benefit is not just lost; the disruption impacts negatively on the entire organisation, and as a result the project is usually pulled or simply left to quietly die.

2. **The technology that provides the means for such social collaboration is frequently outside of the traditional corporate or enterprise IT suite of tools.** As a result, it is often deemed to be unsuitable for use. The irony is that in most cases it is the business that is driving the need for social collaboration and the challenge is to help the IT department to evolve from their old approach, formed over the past 30 years, and to relinquish control. IT departments have often worked hard to establish safety and structure. Enabling collaboration to flow fast and free can feel counter to that. Nevertheless, the recent trend of the consumerisation of IT, led by a new wave of devices and a much richer personal experience, has set the precedent. As we'll see shortly, this is but the beginning – IT departments and the businesses they serve are going to have to seek a happy medium where the evolving, dynamic needs of the business can be matched by the cost-effective deployment and management of its IT services.

3. Finally, and most significantly, it comes down to **the risk of democratisation.** Concerns will be felt at all levels about the risk of people using social tools inappropriately. And it's the tools, more than the people, that will be doubted. Yet

while flattened hierarchies and fluid collaboration present risks, these risks remain fundamentally in the hands of the individuals that use them. If you can't trust employees with these tools, you can hardly trust them without them. We see this debate play out every day in our newspapers, where journalists decry the abuse of technology and usually end up with a call to ban or switch off the technology. In the face of the cultural change needed to minimise the risks of a social business, many firms shy away. It feels safer to hide behind familiar technology and processes. But while it may be easier, it is never safer.

AN UNSTOPPABLE WAVE

Even if half-hearted implementation or outright fear have turned many a business away from becoming authentically social, it is a business revolution that very few will be able to ignore. It's something of an unstoppable wave. There are two allied trends behind this.

1. The first is the next stage in the consumerisation of IT. Instead of the focus being on devices, it is increasingly being placed upon the *services* that we use to incredible effect in our personal lives. This is only going to sharpen the desire to be able to take advantage of this functionality and sharing inside the workplace.

2. The second is essentially a series of technology mega trends – social, mobile and location, cloud, identity and personalisation – all powered by the biggest, most hyped and arguably most transformative trend of all: big data.

The second generation of IT consumerisation should not be underestimated. It starts simply with employees seeking to use the same tools and platforms in the workplace as they use at home. For example, council-run libraries looking to use the familiarity and interconnectedness of Facebook to build a community around their service. But it doesn't end there. It ends with employees looking to use the *principles* that underpin social collaboration across the entirety of their business.

Open government data has changed the way in which citizens both have access to, and can innovate with, government resources. The same effects can be felt on a micro level inside businesses when access to all the different organisational silos is opened up to any employee.

The other key element of the second generation of the consumerisation is a clash of collaborative cultures. When we use most social tools in our personal lives our primary starting position for collaboration is to be "open". We are predisposed to sharing first. We seek to keep certain information private second (although admittedly we are still coming to terms with where that line should be drawn). In business, it's almost always been the other way round. Knowledge is power for the individual who holds it. So in most firms, the default collaborative state is to be closed, opening access only where required (or forced).

As more and more people enter businesses with collaborative expectations set by what is possible in their personal lives, friction is inevitably going to occur. Disruption will follow until a happy balance can be found.

Don't be fooled into thinking that this is an age-based anomaly – something caused by younger generations joining the workforce. The use of social may be more extreme in younger generations. But it is significant across *every* age group of internet-connected individuals. The more socially powerful services pervade our personal lives, the greater our expectations will be that we can harness them – or their principles – at work.

Ultimately, this *should* be the IT department's dream situation. For the first time, their (internal) customers are reaching out for more. They know instinctively that technology is capable of revolutionising work and they want help to bring it about. This is a long way from IT departments having to persuade businesses about the value of "email" or "networks".

VIRTUAL COFFEE

Video-conferencing offers an embryonic example of the impact of the second generation of IT consumerisation – people getting better at adapting services to their needs, and carrying that through into business.

Compared to a few years ago, collaborating via video link is pretty straightforward now. There is no longer any need for massive video-conferencing suites costing thousands. Software such as Skype, in combination with built-in cameras on most laptops and mobile devices, makes video chat in business easy and acceptable.

It doesn't have to stop there, though. In fact, fairly common discomfort with video-calling suggests that it can't if the full benefits are to be felt. Quite a lot of people actually prefer to turn the video feed off. The technology is in place but the human element of the equation isn't comfortable with it.

Mike Dean of Accenture has developed a sophisticated way of using video that not only gets round this but actually makes it a much more useful experience for all concerned. He uses video links regularly to keep in touch with his teams of consultants and outsourcing staff across the UK and the globe. But he makes sure they are much more than long-distance meetings or telephone calls where people stare awkwardly at a little picture of themselves on a screen for an hour.

'We have to make sure that we have a different etiquette for video meetings,' he explains. 'So the first five minutes of all my longer video meetings are used just to catch up like you normally do around the coffee machine. "How are you?" "What's happening?" "How was the weekend?" Because that's the stuff that gets missed; and it really makes a difference.'

He has also instigated 'virtual coffee slots' with his teams in Bangalore or Manila once a quarter. 'It's not a meeting. We just get together. They're on the video link, and we all get a coffee or lunch depending what time of day it is, and we just talk about the cricket – the stuff that you would do if you were in the same office. You get to know a little bit about people's backgrounds. It helps to get the collaborative culture right.'

EVERYTHING TOGETHER

The point here is that Mike Dean has to implement these ideas because there is still quite a lot of friction in the system. It is not a seamless experience switching on your video application. It is even less seamless to use it in a relaxed fashion. It all takes a bit of effort. Fortunately the technology behind social collaboration in business is itself getting ever more frictionless.

Harald Becker, a senior business strategist at Microsoft Office Labs Envisioning Group, sees a future, not that far off, when social technologies will be profoundly more integrated with everything else.

> 'In many ways, for example, video is still a disconnected service from the work that people do. It requires people to switch modes. They have to open up another app, get into another mindset. It takes them out of their flow.'

The future, Harald says, should be different. It should be better. 'You ought to be able to work on live content. For that, I don't have to open up Microsoft Word or Microsoft Excel. It's simply live content that I am working on. And while I'm working on it, I should be able to share it without having to go off somewhere else. I should be able to have a quick IM conversation about it from *within* it. Or I should be able to turn what I'm doing into a video call if I'm so inclined. We're seeing an evolutionary path towards integrative experiences like this – where stuff comes together into the creative work flow, rather than having the work flow dotted around the place in different parcels. The machine will support us and not the other way round.'

JUST THE WAY THINGS ARE

The future implications for social are immense. I'm pretty sure that soon the idea of a business that does not use social tools will seem strange and anachronistic.

Yammer's Mike Grafham sums it up: 'For me the ultimate sign of social's success will be when people will stop using the phrase "social business". It will simply be part of the way you do your work. We don't talk about telephone business or email business. Social will be just a channel for getting things done.'

But perhaps the last word on the power of open, collaborative networks within your business should come from the US military – an unexpected endorsement from what you would expect to be a bastion of closed hierarchical communication. But General Stanley McChrystal, who ran Joint Special Operations Command in Iraq and Afghanistan for nearly five years and later commanded all US and international forces in Afghanistan, told *Fast Company* that the threat of Al-Qaeda forced him to rethink the rules.

> 'We had to change our structure, to become a network. We were required to react quickly. Instead of decisions being made by people who were more senior – the assumption that senior meant wiser – we found that the wisest decisions were usually made by those closest to the problem.'

Being social is a way to free up the potential of workers and to make businesses infinitely more agile. But it also requires, as McChrystal points out, a change in management attitude. And this vital need to change – lurking behind everything we've discussed so far – is what we will deal with in the next chapter.

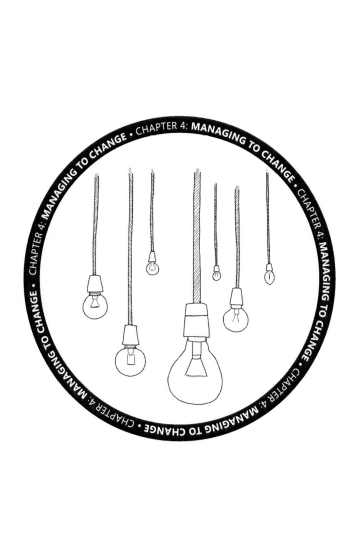

REVOLUTION IN A SLIDE SHOW

NETFLIX HAS COME a long way since it was founded in 1997 by Reed Hastings and his partners as a DVD-by-mail company in the US. Today it's a disc rental and video-streaming company with 30 million subscribers worldwide. Oh, and it's just started making its own TV programmes.

The CEO of Netflix recently took to Facebook to announce that its subscribers watched four billion streaming hours of video in three months. Some say that one of the pillars of the company's success has been its culture and innovative management style. Netflix wanted to attempt to retain the ability to grow big without losing entrepreneurial spirit and flexibility. It did this in a pretty gutsy way.

The company's culture has been codified in a SlideShare presentation that has become a Silicon Valley cultural manifesto – dubbed by Facebook COO Sheryl Sandberg as possibly 'the most important document ever to come out of the Valley'. The presentation, called "Freedom and Responsibility" was first posted publicly in 2009 and has been regularly updated. It is said to have been viewed more than three million times.

So what are the founding principles of Netflix's culture? It is a sharp rebuttal to the hierarchical structures of the old way of managing people. It puts creativity at the heart of the business and places a huge amount of trust in the employees to work for the good of the company:

> 'Our model is to increase employee freedom as we grow, rather than limit it, so that we continue to attract and nourish innovative people so that we have a better chance of sustained success.'

Perhaps Netflix's most famous injunction is over holiday entitlement:

> 'Netflix Vacation Policy and Tracking. There is no policy or tracking.'

Employees are left to themselves to work out how much holiday they should take. Similarly, Netflix's expenses policy consists of five words: 'Act in Netflix's Best Interest.'

The logic of Netflix's culture is contained in four particular slides:

Process Brings Seductively Strong Near-Term Outcome

- A highly-successful process-driven company
  - With leading share in its market
  - Minimal thinking required
  - Few mistakes made – very efficient
  - Few curious innovator-mavericks remain
  - Very optimized processes for its existing market
  - Efficiency has trumped flexibility

51

The logic of Netflix's culture in four slides

Then the Market Shifts...

- Market shifts due to new technology or competitors or business models
- Company is unable to adapt quickly
  - because the employees are extremely good at following the existing processes, and process adherence is the value system
- Company generally grinds painfully into irrelevance

52

Seems Like Three Bad Options

1. Stay creative by staying small, but therefore have less impact
2. Avoid rules as you grow, and suffer chaos
3. Use process as you grow to drive efficient execution of current model, but cripple creativity, flexibility, and ability to thrive when your market eventually changes

53

A Fourth Option

- Avoid Chaos as you grow with Ever More High Performance People – not with Rules
  - Then you can continue to mostly run informally with self-discipline, and avoid chaos
  - The run informally part is what enables and attracts creativity

54

In other words, Netflix wants to tolerate a large amount of uncertainty. It is asking its employees to go for "risk" over workplace stability and its managers to be far more open and un-hierarchical than is traditional. If an employee does something wrong, it is seen as a failure of communication by the manager who has improperly set the context for the badly completed task.

Netflix admits that this is not for everyone:

> 'Many people love our culture, and stay a long time. They thrive on excellence and candour and change ... Some people, however, value job security over performance, and don't like our culture.'

Individual success is measured by what great work is accomplished, not by hours worked or what time employees arrive in the office. But it can be brutal – even employees who perform at an adequate B level due to hard work and effort are rewarded with 'a generous severance package, with respect', so the company can hire an A-player in their place.

High performers are so valued because, according to the manifesto:

> 'In procedural work, the best are 2x better than the average. In creative / inventive work, the best are 10x better.'

Critics have argued that Netflix's relentless focus on high performers is unrealistic and a recipe for chaos within large companies. Whatever the truth of that, Netflix has proved itself adroit at understanding market changes. It has gone from a DVD delivery service to a powerhouse of online video streaming and content creation, satisfying consumer demands by taking advantage of rapidly improving technology and marketplace revolutions.

THE DEATH OF HIERARCHY

Netflix's culture is still a relatively rare example of a company that has grasped the need to respond to the speed of change engendered by the technology revolution.

We have discussed how collaboration, flexibility and the democratisation of the workplace can play a huge part in how business can be reimagined for the better. But it is not enough to stop there.

It is necessary also to change the culture of the company and the way that employers and employees, manager and the managed, interact. Companies and workers need to be optimised by output not by the standardisation of process.

Harald Becker, a senior business strategist at Microsoft Office Labs Envisioning Group, explains:

'At the end of the day, if you look at what makes up an effective collaboration environment, technology is really only one piece of the puzzle. It's often culture that stands in the way. It does not support how people work together. You can have the best tools in the world, but if your management culture does not support sharing and collaboration, they won't do you any good.'

This is a key point. As we discovered in Chapter 1, although technology is obviously an enabler of success, it is not the solution alone.

THE END OF EFFICIENCY

One of the main drivers for the need of this cultural change is the arrival in the workplace of *millenials*. These are people born roughly between 1977 and 1997 and they go by several names – digital natives, the net generation, generation Y.

Whatever you call them, they have grown up with ever-advancing technology and networked collaboration. And this means they are *much* less likely to accept old hierarchical structures and the delayed career gratification of the 20th century. They want more freedom, openness and less structure.

Never has a generation entered the workplace using technologies so far ahead of those generally adopted by the firms employing them. Chief among these, as we have discussed, is the ability to connect with anyone anywhere – either to communicate or to collaborate. Of course, this also means it is possible today to hire and integrate talent from across the world – the competition for the best brains is fiercer than ever before.

But we would do well to avoid the easy trap of thinking that all of this is therefore only applicable to younger generations. You only have to look at key social-networking platforms like Facebook and Twitter to see that a significant portion of their user base is made up of those who precede the millenials. Social is not just for "kids". It is widely used across all ages. And it is changing *everyone's* expectations.

All this demands a response in the way businesses empower and engage their employees, no matter the profile of their average employee.

Because management, facing these changes, looks very broken right now. In *The Future of Management* Gary Hamel crystalises this problem:

'To a large extent managers play the role of parents, school principles, crossing guards and hall monitors. They employ control from without because employees have been deprived of the ability to exercise control from within. Adolescents outgrow most of these constraining influences; employees often aren't give the chance. The result: disaffection. Adults enjoy being treated like 13-year-olds even less than 13-year-olds.'

Yammer founder Adam Pisoni is particularly focused on how the old management obsessions no longer make much sense:

'Companies were designed to optimise for efficiency. That made sense in a world where the pace of change was relatively slow, and organisations could, in turn, institute rigid structure and processes across the business to accomplish one specific task as quickly as possible. By doing the same thing for a relatively long period of time, companies who offered similar products or services essentially just competed on efficiency.

'In order to do something in the most efficient way, companies were also extremely reliant on the notion of predictability. Success was governed by predicting challenges, training employees to respond to these expected outcomes, and ultimately rewarding predictability. So businesses thrived on a hierarchal structure with a calibre that flows up, leading to really narrow job descriptions.

'The name of the game is: "Let's make sure we know what everybody is doing at every moment, and employees will follow instructions and execute in exactly the right way – and then we'll just keep driving efficiency."

'In a world where what matters is predictability and efficiency, you don't want your employees to take it upon themselves to be innovative or creative. You want them executing specific, job-oriented tasks.

'Then something changed. To be fair, it's been happening for about 50 years but more noticeably in the last ten or 20. The pace of disruption and change exceeded the ten-year mark. It blew past the five-year mark. And suddenly all of the work that went into making companies efficient not only became irrelevant because you're not going to be doing it long enough for it to matter but it actually became counterproductive. In trying to do things efficiently, you are inherently not adaptable.

'When all of the old rules fall apart, all the what's the role of the employee? What's the role of a manager? What's the point of a hierarchy? All of that starts to fall down because these standards were designed for a world that didn't change very quickly.'

So the fundamental question becomes: how do we organise work better to take this into account? What does an effective business culture look like?

MANAGEMENT REIMAGINED

The traditional way of forming a company is when a group of people come together to provide something of value, to meet some demand. What often happens in this process is that providing value and the *way* that value is provided sooner or later gets confused. The former is essential (it's why people come to you). The latter is ultimately only incidental.

As Yammer's Adam Pisoni elaborates: 'In every single case, the *way* that your customers want you to fulfil that demand will change. This was always the case, but today it's happening faster. However, since we confuse the value that we offer with the way we offer it, we miss out. We begin to spin our wheels trying to get better and better at the way that we provided the value.'

In other words, businesses need to be organised from top to bottom around the value they provide. They have to be good at the process of providing it – but that process is not their value. And this is true today more than ever.

Employees' and managers' roles should be defined by the *value* they provide as part of the *company's value*. Their job descriptions should be completely formed around it. And then they should be asked – and empowered – to innovate in how they provide it.

Pisoni goes on to bring up the interesting example of Blockbuster, a rival to Netflix. Unlike Netflix, Blockbuster failed to adapt to changing market conditions and consumer demands. But not in the way you would expect.

'The value Blockbuster offered was based on the fact that people wanted to watch movies at home. The way they offered that value – which was the best possible way in 1985 – was to have physical stores where you could rent VHS tapes. The whole company was organised around that way of delivering this specific value; people's job descriptions were written based on parts of profit in that value chain.

'As broadband internet became a part of our lives, customers wanted that value delivered in a different way. People wanted to download or stream movies because it was a better and easier way of watching movies at home. But Blockbuster was blind to this changing demand. They'd begun to confuse the value they provided with *how* they provided it. Because of that, they couldn't adapt.

'People often think businesses get disrupted because they don't improve. But Blockbuster actually improved rapidly. They eliminated late fees, which was ground-breaking at the time. They expanded the potential for a home cinema experience by offering food. They came up with all sorts of ways to improve the value they offered. But none of it mattered, because they'd gotten it wrong. They weren't actually improving the value that they *truly* offered: watching movies at home. They were improving a particular delivery mechanism for that value. They were improving a *way* of providing value. It wasn't good enough.'

In order to avoid a colossal mistake like Blockbuster's, business leaders must have the confidence to let go of the command and controls. Fortunately, this isn't as frightening as it sounds. Autonomy actually becomes an intrinsic motivator for the employee – they feel trusted with freedom, empowered to be creative and to innovate.

In this world the role of the manager also changes – they are no longer the definer of process, the hander out of minute-by-minute instructions. In this new scenario, it is simply their job to:

- make sure that everybody's aligned on the company's mission

- measure the output of the company

- make sure that the right incentives are in place so that people are motivated to make the best decisions and be creative.

Benjamin Ellis, British social technologist and entrepreneur, emphasises the importance of alignment:

'It's the critical difference between efficiency and effectiveness, and the biggest challenge in a distributed environment. Which of these is better: one person achieving one thing that moves the business towards a strategic objective, or 100 people each doing ten things towards five irrelevant goals?

' "Anti-work" is corrosive to a business, and yet in survey after survey, I find workers either don't know what the goals of their business are, or are working towards an outdated definition of them.

'Clearly set and communicated goals allow people to work interdependently and flexibly. Goals need to be broken down into meaningful steps so there is an objective way to establish if things are going awry.

'If people know where they are going, they will get there – provided they are motivated.'

CREATIVE MANAGEMENT CULTURE

So what does creative management culture look like in practice? Below are three different and equally fascinating examples: from Yammer, Grey London and Zappos.

Yammer

'I'm a manager at a company that moves really fast,' says Yammer's Adam Pisoni. 'It moves too fast for me to assume that I can pop into a particular team project and begin turning dials and really change things. I'd just be slowing it down. And if people have to go through me for approval to change stuff themselves, it's still too slow.'

Instead, he explains,

> 'what I do is I look at the aggregate output of my team of engineers: how is our velocity, what is the quality like? And I don't try to fix that (if it needs fixing) by going to a person in the traditional management way. I ask myself: "Are people aligned?" In other words, do people understand what value they're providing – are they concentrating on what matters to the overall business – and do they have the right framework for making decisions?

> 'If they don't, it's important to spend a lot of energy on that. The second question I ask is: "What can I change about our process to improve the things that matter to me like velocity?" And so we spend a lot of time at Yammer adjusting the process. But it's outcome-focused and it's very lightweight.

'My job as a leader is to create alignment so people understand the direction we're going. But everyone at the company has to have autonomy for us to work at this pace. They may do things differently than I would have done it, but that's okay – as long as the output is good.'

Grey London

Grey London is a communications agency who initiated a corporate culture regime called Open. This has deconstructed the traditional notions of hierarchy to foster greater collaboration both internally and externally.

Managers at Grey London have become coaches and cultural guardians, and employees are celebrated as agents of great work. Management sign-offs have been removed in many cases to ensure greater speed. The agency claims that this new environment – now four years old – is the best way to create fantastic creative solutions and happy clients. It's been, they say, 'the engine behind our new business success which has seen us nearly double in size'.

The key to this change is *democratisation* of information and a flatter, faster company hierarchy.

Zappos

This democratisation is something that online shoe and apparel company Zappos have focused on strongly too. Tony Hsieh, CEO of Zappos, explained their thinking to WorldBlu (**www. worldblu.com**), a global network of organisations committed to practising freedom and democracy in the workplace.

'A democratic workplace for us equals happiness. We choose to practise democracy in the workplace because it not only blurs the line between managers and employees but it also drives the distribution of power, encourages innovation, and helps attract the best talent. It is important that any employee, from our call centre to our executive team, has the ability to make changes that impact how the organisation operates, develops, and grows.'

This has a number of implications, Hsieh says:

'Our call centre employees are not required to read from scripts because we want to empower them to service our customer in the best way they can – in a way that is suited for that customer. We also want to see employees at all levels make decisions without having to get a manager or supervisor involved. Running the organisation with a lot of freedom offers our employees the time to collaborate and get work done but have fun doing it.'

EDUCATING SELF-DIRECTION

Of course, democratised workplaces can be challenging for employees. It's not always easy to take on more responsibility. Autonomy can be scary and stressful. If poorly implemented, such a leap in culture runs the risk of cutting employees adrift in a sea of new responsibility, without the skills to cope with it and without adequate direction from managers.

This also has implications for how we teach people to think about what work is. Helping our children to develop the right skills to take advantage of a new flexible, creative workplace almost certainly means questioning the regimented nature of school and university. Will it adequately prepare a future generation for the kind of world on its way?

The structured approach to education mimics that of the workplace. You start at the bottom, you attend the same location at the same time as everyone else, you follow a pre-determined path of processes (lessons split by topics) and over the years you progress to greater levels of both skill and status within the organisation. Differing levels of individual capability aside, this process is on rails. It's pretty tough to deviate from. It provides structure and direction, which is important in the early years, but in the later stages this can be prescriptive – constraining the individual's ability to grow and innovate.

Furthermore, it does little to prepare individuals for a world of self-direction. This is perhaps easier within higher education, but far too often even there things still revolve around a similar hierarchy to that found in the offices of today (and of the last 100 years) – a group of individuals directed by a single leader.

If we want to reap the benefits of the reimagined business, we need to equip the future workforce with the cognitive skills that will ensure their success.

This really means teaching them about skills *not* tools. Rather than teaching children how to use word processors, or keyboards, or mice, or web pages (all stuff they will teach themselves), we need to teach them critical thinking – how to stay safe online, how to communicate responsibly and effectively, how to search and reference, and so on. The way we currently teach technology just reinforces the problem of humans failing to live up to the potential technology offers.

ENGAGING EVERYONE

'It turns out that if you begin to take away bureaucracy, trust is the currency you use. You exchange bureaucracy for trust. And trust is a currency that can actually drive agility.'

– ADAM PISONI, YAMMER

If everyone shares the same view of the challenges and objectives of the business, and individuals are freed and incentivised to find the best way to achieve the right outcomes using all their skills and experience (rather than their competence in completing a prescribed process), things change.

Some have even described the new working experience as addictive. With engaged employees and managers, a virtuous circle takes hold. Indeed, there is little doubt about the statistical importance of engaging employees and the effect that it has on performance. Studies have shown that engagement has a measurable impact on innovation, customer service and retention, to name but a few areas.

Little wonder then that a CBI Harvey Nash employment trends survey in 2012 found that securing high levels of employee engagement was the top workforce priority for UK businesses, ahead even of containing labour costs.

As consulting firm BlessingWhite found in a report on workplace engagement: 'Engaged employees plan to stay for what they give. The disengaged stay for what they get.' On a similar note, Lynda Gratton in her seminal book *The Shift: The Future of Work is Already Here* makes the striking point that the formula for the traditional deal at work runs as follows:

> 'I work ... to earn money ... which I use ... to consume stuff ... which makes me happy.'

She suggests that in future this should be:

> 'I work ... to gain productive experiences ... that are the basis ... of my happiness.'

She is right – and it should be true for executives, managers and the managed. In a reimagined business, workers are measured on outputs, given full access to information and empowered to make their own decisions by managers who have let go of bureaucracy and embraced transparency and trust.

This makes for far happier employees and a far more productive business. With only 30% of workers feeling engaged today (as we saw earlier), the time to change how we do business has got to be now.

'People ask me to predict the future, when all I want to do is prevent it. Better yet, build it. Predicting the future is much too easy, anyway. You look at the people around you, the street you stand on, the visible air you breathe, and predict more of the same. To hell with more. I want better.'

– RAY BRADBURY

BEAUTIFUL BUT USELESS

A T HOME, ON my kitchen table, there sits a colourful disc of paper. The disc is beautifully printed, ornate in its detail, and upon its face it bears a large printed calendar date, accompanied by a small personalised inscription.

The paperwork in question is, of course, the replacement tax disc for my car and it has languished on my kitchen table for almost a month, beguiling me with both its beauty and its sheer irrelevance in today's world. It is a great example of the challenge businesses find themselves facing, how they need to develop products that are relevant to their customers and live up to the potential of our modern, digital society.

The Driver and Vehicle Licensing Agency (DVLA) owns and curates the vehicle register, a database of vehicles and vehicle tax. The folks at the DVLA know when my tax is due and they lovingly remind me, and explain easy ways to pay. They also make this database available to law-enforcement agencies and the insurance industry, and in conjunction with a national system of cameras culminating in the ANPR (Automatic Number Plate Recognition) system they have removed the need for the bobby on the beat to run around peering into car windows looking for out-of-date pieces of colourful paper.

The ornate discs behind millions of windscreens lie unseen, unappreciated and unused – a remnant of a time long gone by (the tax disc was introduced in 1921), a curious paper artefact, a reminder of our analogue past.

In a world where we seem to be clutching at straws for new ways to minimise costs, I am left wondering just how much inefficiency, effort and spend is tied up in processes like this that have long since passed their point of relevance in how we behave. My bet is that you all have your own example of the DVLA's tax disc. You simply need the confidence and open-mindedness to ask "What if we could do things differently?" – "What might our business look like then?"

In the DVLA's case there is hopefully a happy ending. The DVLA has conducted a national consultation with the stated aim of getting rid of the paper tax disc. Officials confirmed that most on-road enforcement action is now based on the ANPR system and the number plate rather than by visual inspection of the tax disc. It was said that going completely digital would save businesses, including vehicle fleet operators, huge sums of money by not having to handle the administration of tax discs – not to mention the massive saving to the state in not having to create and administer their distribution and renewal.

Of course, the British government has to ensure that going digital does not mean a loss of tax revenue, so the final decision has yet to be made. But I am hopeful. For me it is a great example of a long-established organisation having the imagination and courage to respond to change and rethink the way they do things.

I believe that the need for businesses to reimagine the way they work like this is unarguable and will be the way that organisations compete in the future.

The solution lies in the areas we have discussed: flexible working, going social and management change.

THE DEATH OF DESKS

For many, flexible working is a reality. Working from home, the office or third spaces is happening in companies everywhere. Attitudes towards flexible working are changing: business leaders see the benefits. Recent research found that 77% of chief executives and 54% of senior managers are working flexibly, and 88% and 85% respectively have done so in the past four years.

The study by the Institute of Leadership and Management surveyed more than 1,000 organisations across several sectors in the UK. It defined flexible working as 'a set of practices which give employees flexibility on how long, where and when they work.' Now, I suspect that in perhaps the majority of the cases, flexible working was being introduced – as discussed in Chapter 2 – as a way of retaining staff. That is, it has been defined almost as a perk for the individual and usually without any cultural change, especially at the middle management layer, which ultimately means benefits will be limited to just a handful of individuals rather than spread throughout the organisation as a whole.

But overall the good news is that change in this area is coming. Technology is making it almost inevitable. We are all working with devices and data streams that connect us within and without the office space and across time zones. Work is just getting an awful lot "lighter". For some a tablet has become their desktop; how much longer can we go on believing they need a desk?

The infrastructure of the workplace has shifted from the physical elements of the office, desk and chair to simply (AC) power, internet access and (if you're lucky) good coffee.

Not to say that office space is dead. Just like the predicted demise of email, communal working space will actually always be necessary – just not in the way in which we use it today.

Places where people can come together are still critical for some aspects of creativity and the sort of relationship-building that oils the wheels of productive work. Which is why "bums on seats" memos can still do the rounds and be roundly misinterpreted. It is interesting to note that some time after the infamous Yahoo! HR memo on working from home, Marissa Mayer felt compelled to point out that she was not speaking on behalf of the industry: 'It was wrongly perceived as an industry narrative.'

The real narrative is that flexible working *must* be a strategic objective for companies looking to profitably reimagine how they do business, whether they want to maintain an office space or not. Companies that take a holistic approach to flexible working will find themselves doing all sorts of healthy things. Above all, by focusing on outcomes not on time served (whether in the office or in Starbucks), they will be empowering employees to make their own choices to play their part in the success of the business. And businesses like that are a lot more successful.

There are implications here beyond what reimagined business means for offices – there will also be changes in the way cities work. Cities will become blended, much more of a mixture of work and living spaces. Jack Dorsey, founder of Twitter, said: 'Having a coffee together is so much more important to creating something than a business meeting'. The point is: getting together creatively for work no longer necessarily means meeting at the office.

Thinking differently about the "built environment" in this way could have substantial benefits in terms of cost savings. We know that most office buildings are grossly under-occupied

– only 30% to 40% of their workspace used in a typical day. And even within that, individuals are spending less and less time at their allocated space, their desk. There are also huge inefficiencies in the time, money and energy spent on commuting (not to mention the detriment of the planet). I am sure that technology and the right sort of cultural change will see us refashion our working lives into a much broader, more sustainable shape.

ORGANISMS RATHER THAN ORGANISATIONS

It is my view that businesses that adopt this thorough, strategic approach to flexible working will not only stand a greater chance of success because they have put in place the necessary cultural and process changes required, they will also have re-established and addressed the key issue of trust with their employees.

This new world of work, where the organisational and informational hierarchies are not just flattened but laid completely open, fundamentally changes the dynamics of a business. It promotes agility and focus around a common objective, effectively creating a malleable, self-healing organisation that can adapt and transform as quickly as the market changes.

It's about being an organism rather than an organisation. Silos and hierarchies are broken down, enabling information, data and decisions to flow faster and more collaboratively than ever before. This enables better, more informed business decisions to be taken.

Mike Grafham of Yammer says that once the benefits of collaborative agility become clear, the competitive advantage will mean there will be no turning back.

'If you embed this network-based way of thinking into how your organisation operates, it does two things. Firstly, it makes you more agile. Secondly, because it's made you more agile, it's going to incrementally make you *better* at being more agile. So you're going to be on this exponential curve of being able to adapt faster than other people,' he says.

'If a company doesn't get on that curve quickly enough, they are going to be left in the dust by all of their competition because the networked businesses will be accelerating away from them.'

It is more difficult to predict some of the other business effects of breaking down the communications silos. But some of the hints of what is possible are pretty exciting.

One company introduced Yammer into its business and produced one much-unexpected side effect – a complete change in the way the chairman related to the company. Here is what happened in the CEO's own words. (To spare the company's blushes, I have anonymised some of the details.)

> 'Our chairman would come in once a quarter to the board meetings and I would talk to him on a reasonably regular basis; maybe once every couple of weeks we'd have a chat on the phone and I would update him on how the organisation was going, what we were doing, some of the key things that were happening.

'Then we gave him access to Yammer. One of the things I'd never even thought of was how I used to manage the information that he received through regular emails, telephone calls and board meetings. I kept a pretty tight grip on the flow of what he used to know about. Soon I was getting phone calls from him because he was accessing much more information from the Yammer groups that he was signed up to.

'Now he had access to everything that was going on in the company without it being managed. Some might expect this to be a major headache but in fact it has transformed the way he has been able to contribute to the company. Now he has that freedom of information, his contribution to the business is completely different – and much more fulfilling for us as an organisation and for him than it was previously.'

What all this adds up to is a new way of thinking; a flatter hierarchy, a culture of openness.

Transparency and trust in the workplace are the hallmarks of the reimagined business. In the world of flexible working, where the workforce is dispersed, it becomes even more important to build trust through increased communication.

Managers who have employees working from home or on the move will need to find mechanisms to establish trust from the start. Perhaps a set amount of time together is necessary. Mike Dean of Accenture recounts the practice of remote workers who spend time when in the office "doing the rounds" of co-workers. Relationships like this are the key to trust.

THE KNOWLEDGE OF EVERY JOB

But there will be those who are thinking: "This is all very well. This is all very utopian. But this sort of reimagining is not for me; it is not for my business."

The honest answer to this is that there are some industries and professions where the sort of changes we are discussing are less relevant and will take longer to penetrate. But I find it hard to subscribe to the argument that says that all that we have discussed here is restricted only to knowledge workers.

Every single job requires and creates knowledge. The trick for all businesses is not just to recognise that but to harness it. Who knows better about the best (and worst) ways of operating a specific element of the production line than those operating it every single day? Who better understands the opportunities and challenges of the front-of-house service in retail or airport security than those performing those duties?

These individuals have struggled to become part of their employer's knowledge economy in the past – but only because they didn't spend time behind a computer screen, or the systems couldn't adapt to allow their input (or their management wouldn't allow them a voice).

Opportunities like flexible working and the democratisation of the workforce, combined with a digital society where most people are using collaborative technology instinctively in their personal lives, mean that organisations can finally tap into that wisdom and experience. At long last, those insights that have been hidden for so long can be turned into a rich source of innovation.

All businesses need to do is to open up the channels of collaboration and adapt their concepts of management and control to enable it to happen. Above all, they need to align employees not to compartmentalised processes but to the company's overall objectives. We could all learn from JFK's visit to NASA in 1962; when the president happened to ask the janitor what he was doing, the janitor simply replied: 'I'm helping to put man on the moon'.

THE POTENTIAL OF THE FUTURE

If you're still with me (and thanks for getting this far) you're hopefully inspired by the potential of the future world of work. I suspect you may also be frustrated by the fact there aren't enough answers here to help you make it happen tomorrow. The truth is, the answers are hard. More importantly, the specifics are different for every organisation.

But if your head is full of questions now, that's probably a good sign you're ready to play your own part in reimagining business. Thankfully there is something straightforward I think you can do that will help those answers to come.

Throughout this book, I hope I have shown that reimagining business is not about the individual importance of activities such as flexible working, being social and the management of change. It is about the incredible effects that can be achieved when these three are *brought together* and thought about collectively.

The successful businesses of the future will combine these elements to empower their employees within the context of their overall business goals. This engagement will in turn reinforce and engender trust and responsibility. Such trust and responsibility will become the crucible from which agility, innovation and success will follow.

The flip side of this is that if organisations continue on as they are doing now, I believe they are setting themselves up for increased inflexibility and friction, reducing the extent to which they innovate and remain competitive. By not addressing the potential of these issues across the entire organisation, by continuing to collaborate in hierarchical and organisational silos, and managing rather than leading, such organisations are falling victim to inertia. They end up with a disengaged workforce, which will reduce the company's ability to adapt, react and innovate.

BEING BRAVE

Some sceptics might say that it is all very well for someone who works for a technology company like Microsoft to preach the importance of the sort of innovations that reflect many of Microsoft's products. But, like I said, technology alone is not the answer.

The truth is that, while Microsoft is deeply embedded in the big technology trends of cloud, big data, mobile and social, it is only one company among quite a few. These changes are happening right now and my role at Microsoft simply means it is my privilege to have a ringside seat. Like all others, Microsoft is on a journey to the future of work. In some respects it is ahead of the game; in other respects there is a way to go.

My purpose in writing this book has been to start a proper conversation about the future of work, given these seismic changes in technology and the workplace. I am enthused by the potential that lies at our fingertips. But I am frustrated by how hard it is for us to live up to that potential. Instead of an impossible one-size-fits-all step-by-step guide, ultimately I wanted this to be the beginning of a dialogue about how we might figure this out together.

So my challenge to you is this. I know that if you've picked up this book, you've probably shared that nagging sense of doubt about the fact that we're not achieving all we could in the 21st century workplace. I also know you will probably have examples of the potential for this sort of change inside your business. Don't get me wrong, I'm often naively optimistic but I'm not stupid. I'm not saying that *everything* inside your business can (or needs to) be changed. But if you take a long, hard look at the processes that surround you and ask yourself (and your teams) the simple question "Why do we do this like this?" and you *ever* hear the answer, "Because we've always done it like that", then you know that you've probably found the beginnings of something that needs to be rethought.

Make no mistake, in order to do this you're going to have to do some really difficult things. You're going to have to be brave. You've got to think differently about the future.

TALKING TO YOUR APPLIANCES

Kids are naturals at this because their expectations are much less bound up by past experiences. They don't spend their time thinking about what *won't* happen, only what *might*. They haven't developed that cynical inner voice we curate as adults, the one that gently whispers "Oh no, that will never work" at the threshold of every new idea.

I have a seven-year-old son and he is a constant reminder of the importance of thinking openly about what might be possible before you start thinking about why it isn't. I had a wonderful experience of this a couple of years ago. We were doing some work with Channel 4 News about voice recognition as part of Microsoft's launch of the Xbox Kinect – the add-on camera device that also allows the Xbox 360 to be controlled by gestures and your voice. It was a big deal and we were all very excited.

The night before the interview I had the beta software up and running at home. Like the dutiful corporate spokesperson that I am, I did all my homework ready for the interview the next day – that is to say, my son and I were playing on the Xbox in the name of "research". We spent an hour together barking commands at the TV, like 'Xbox play this DVD', 'Xbox play this game'. Each time, the console calmly obeyed and my son loved it.

After a while, he stopped and ran off. And then I heard this little voice from the kitchen saying: 'Microwave – make my tea'. Moments later it was followed by a cry for help: 'Dad, the microwave's bust.'

These are the moments of magic that should open our eyes to what might be possible. We shouldn't think about how the world is today, but instead about how the world might be if we did things differently.

This is easier said than done, but the memorable examples out there of people failing to do it ought to help spur us on.

Jonathan Margolis brilliantly captured the problem in his book *A Brief History of Tomorrow*. He identified the 'arrogance of the present' – that we can't measure the future value of anything easily because we measure it in today's money, today's mind-set.

A classic example of this, Margolis writes, is one incident in the life of American industrialist Henry Ford. He went to the Bank of Michigan in 1903 and spoke to its president. He wanted money to build his factory so he could make cars. But the president turned him down. 'The horse,' he explained, 'is here to stay; but the automobile is only a novelty – a fad.'

Perhaps an even more poignant example – again from the history of the automobile – is the infamous red flag laws of the late 19th century. Did you know that for 30 years in Victorian England, someone was legally obliged to walk in front of any moving car with a red flag?

It seems ridiculous now that you would want to restrict a vehicle to the walking pace of a man. But when the red flag laws were passed in Great Britain (and similar laws were also passed in the US), legislators were thinking about the present and not about the possibilities of the future.

These measures were later reduced but only effectively repealed in 1896, the same year that Karl Benz designed and patented the first internal-combustion engine, called the *boxermotor*.

I always remember the red flag laws when I hear talk of fears about the internet, social networking and the negative effects of the advance of technology. The arrogance of the present is a sort of constraining fear. It says that we've got everything that we need. Anything extra is dangerous. Or could be.

We have to get past this and indulge in a little bit of imagination.

What would we do if the world was different? What could happen if we *did* measure by outcomes, if we *did* empower people to be thoughtful about where they work? If we *did* stop worrying about processes and looked a bit more at our goals?

The key message underneath all of this is empowerment. Technology is here to empower people. But that doesn't work if human structures, habits or fears constrain them. If businesses won't let their employees be free, they'll be doing the 21st-century equivalent of trotting in front of a car waving a length of scarlet cotton.

And their competitors in the fast lane will wave to them as thcy pass.

Acknowledgements

IT IS PERHAPS fitting that a book about the future of collaboration should be the product of the collective passion and wisdom offered by a huge range of people. Everyone we interviewed or simply sought counsel from became an integral part of this book's journey. No contribution was insignificant; even the smallest gestures, comments or ideas opened the door to something larger.

In particular, I'd like to thank Harald Becker, Jo Burkill, Matt Cameron, Linda Chandler, Tony Crabbe, Mike Dean, the DVLA, Benjamin Ellis, Chantal Gautier, Mike Grafham, Ben Hammersley, Damian Horner, Jimmy Leach, Anne McCrossan, Richard Patterson, Adam Pisoni, Nicola Rabson, Philip Ross, Tiffany St James and the team at Yammer for taking the time to help me better understand the challenges facing businesses today – and tomorrow.

In addition, there are a handful of people who sat at the heart of this project and frankly, without whom I simply wouldn't have made it.

I was incredibly lucky to work closely with two people whose insight, drive, humour and sheer tenacity have taken the mildly obsessive ramblings of a naive, optimistic dreamer and turned them into something tangible, focused and productive.

Nick Morris provided the spark for the beginning of this journey four years ago and has been with me every step of the way since. Like all good friends, he is both supportive and critical where required, ensuring that I never get too far ahead of myself and that as a team we remained focused on enabling the very future we so long to see.

It was through Nick that we found our editor, Mike Harvey, who I have to admit, I was pretty intimidated by when we first met. Not because of anything specific he did or said, but because he is the real deal – focused, professional and *very* smart. Fundamentally, I was worried he might rumble the fact that we were, to an extent, making this up as we went along. In addition to all the things you would expect from a world-class editor, Mike brought an incredible sharpness to the story. He brought out the best in me; then he took my output and made it come alive. As far as I am concerned, he is effectively the closest thing to a magician I'll ever come across.

Without Nick and Mike, this would be a loose set of rambling words on a blog you'd never see. The reality is that they both made their effort on top of already incredibly busy lives and careers and I am indebted to both them and their families for this.

Beyond Nick and Mike, several other people and teams were instrumental in getting us this far.

David Stewart, our librarian at Microsoft, represents the very best example of the crucial role that his profession has played in our society for thousands of years. He connected us to knowledge, ideas and people (and music) to help us get where we needed to be.

David introduced us to Sally Tickner, who in turn introduced us to Myles Hunt and the team at Harriman House, who helped us realise the full potential of our work.

Louise Waller, Kate Falcone, Jess Rowntree and all of the team at Bite Global have been the engine that carried the logistical side of getting this done. They worked in the background to help us establish the platform for our work and crucially, did all this while leaving us to get on with the actual creation.

This may be corny for some, but I'd also like to share my appreciation for the people at Microsoft UK who have tolerated my ambition for this story for many years and ultimately created the cognitive headroom for us to explore something that was not necessarily part of the day job.

Finally, the two people that make me all that I am. For John, who in addition to providing the best possible reason for me to be optimistic and passionate about the importance of setting our future up for success, also gives me the best insight (and material) for all that his world might become.

And behind all of this is Margaret, who has not just supported me throughout the late nights of writing and mental absence while I formed the ideas that became this book, but more importantly has long endured the endless conversations about futures that might be, while she unassumingly deals with the reality of the present – ensuring that both I and my family can achieve all that we hope for in our own future.